HEALTH CARE CAREERS IN 2 YEARS ™

JUMP-STARTING A CAREER IN

MEDICAL TECHNOLOGY

AMIE JANE LEAVITT

ROSEN
PUBLISHING®

New York

Published in 2014 by The Rosen Publishing Group, Inc.
29 East 21st Street, New York, NY 10010

Copyright © 2014 by The Rosen Publishing Group, Inc.

First Edition

Library of Congress Cataloging-in-Publication Data

Leavitt, Amie Jane.
Jump-starting a career in medical technology/Amie Jane Leavitt. — First
edition.
    pages cm. — (Health care careers in 2 years)
Includes bibliographical references and index.
ISBN 978-1-4777-1694-6 (library binding)
1. Medical technology—Vocational guidance. 2. Biomedical technicians—
Vocational guidance. 3. Medical technologists—Vocational guidance. 4.
Laboratory technicians—Vocational guidance. I. Title.
R855.3.L43 2014
610.28023—dc23

2013012396

Manufactured in Malaysia

CPSIA Compliance Information: Batch #W14YA: For further information, contact Rosen Publishing, New York, New York,
at 1-800-237-9932.

CONTENTS

INTRODUCTION

Picture this: a pregnant woman enters a private room at her doctor's office and lies down on an examination table. Soon after, a technician wheels a small machine into the room that looks similar to a computer. It has a modified keyboard, a display monitor, and a corded transducer probe.

The technician introduces herself and sits next to the patient. She carefully guides the transducer probe over the bare skin on the patient's stomach. The procedure is painless. In fact, the patient feels nothing except for the sensation of a rubbery plastic object gliding across her skin. As the probe moves across the patient's stomach, it receives sound waves from her uterus. The sound waves are transmitted to the ultrasound machine and then translated into an image of the woman's baby on the display monitor. This is the first time the woman has ever had an ultrasound, and seeing her baby's image on the screen is a thrilling and emotional experience.

The technician prints a paper copy of the image for the woman to keep as a memento of her baby's first photo. The main purpose of the ultrasound isn't just to print a photo, though. It is to help the doctor monitor the baby's growth and development, detect any problems with the baby, determine the gender of the baby, and more

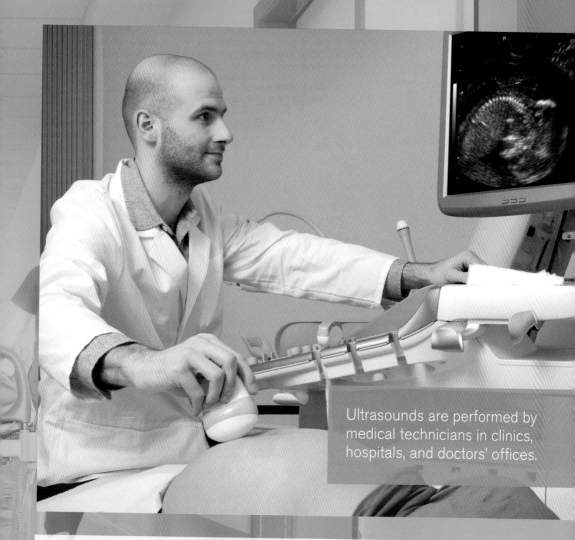

Ultrasounds are performed by medical technicians in clinics, hospitals, and doctors' offices.

accurately predict the woman's due date. In addition to taking ultrasound images of babies in utero, this machine can also take images of other parts of the body, too. This includes muscles, ligaments, joints, the nervous system, the brain, abdominal organs, breasts, and the heart.

Oftentimes, when people think of careers in the medical field, they picture the more commonly known occupations of doctors, surgeons, dentists, and nurses. However, there is definitely much more to the medical field than just these advanced-level positions. In hospitals and clinics, there are people who perform a variety of other jobs. Some take X-rays, MRIs, CAT scans, and ultrasounds, while others watch heart-rate monitors and assist with respiratory and cardiovascular rehabilitation. Some people prepare medical equipment, while others repair that same equipment. Outside a traditional hospital or clinic setting, there are people who work in research laboratories, veterinary offices, dental offices, and ophthalmology offices.

All of these people have two things in common. First, they all work in the field of medical technology. And second, many started their jobs with approximately two years of post–high school education or less.

What draws people into the field of medical technology? The overall attraction seems to be a combined interest in biology and technology and a strong desire to help others. Many people also like the fact that they can work in the medical field without having to spend numerous years and thousands of dollars in medical school. And still others like that they can work in these fields while they are continuing their higher education to become either a doctor or a nurse. Many feel that jobs in medical technology are a great way to get one's foot in the door. This is because there are often opportunities for career advancement in terms of both pay scale and responsibilities with further education (sometimes paid for by the employer) and on-the-job training and experience.

Another reason that people are attracted to the field of medical technology is the projected need for more workers in the coming years in the health care industry. According to the United States Bureau of Labor Statistics' Employment Projections 2010–2020 report: "Industries and occupations related to health care, personal care and social assistance, and construction are projected to have the fastest job growth between 2010 and 2020. . . . Total employment is projected to grow by 14.3 percent over the decade, resulting in 20.5 million new jobs."

So, exactly what are the jobs available in the field of medical technology, and what is it like to work in these jobs? In the next few sections, you'll get a detailed description of some of the jobs available in the field, as well as a selection of in-depth personal interviews with people who are currently employed in the industry. Then you'll find out what education you'll need, how to find a job, and how to climb the health care ladder as a medical technology professional.

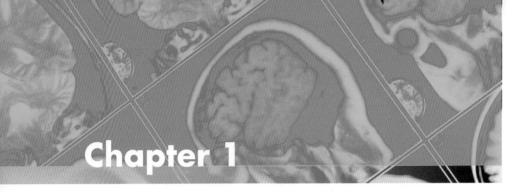

Chapter 1

Using Technology to Diagnose Illness

Even though most people immediately think of doctors and nurses when they hear "health care career," there are a wide variety of other fulfilling, enriching, and vitally important career paths available in the health care industry. And many of them require no more than two years of education (sometimes considerably less!) to get a foot in the door and land that first job.

Diagnostic Medical Technicians

The technician described in the introduction who helped the woman see the image of her baby for the first time is a diagnostic medical technician, or sonographer. This professional uses special imaging equipment, called an ultrasound, to diagnose and assess certain medical conditions or situations.

There are also jobs for sonographers outside traditional hospital or clinical settings. Some people, like sonographer Wendy Reynolds, no longer work in patient care. Instead, she works for an ultrasound manufacturing

After they finish training, diagnostic medical technicians can find work in a variety of capacities within the medical field. They can work directly in patient care or for ultrasound manufacturing companies testing new equipment and software.

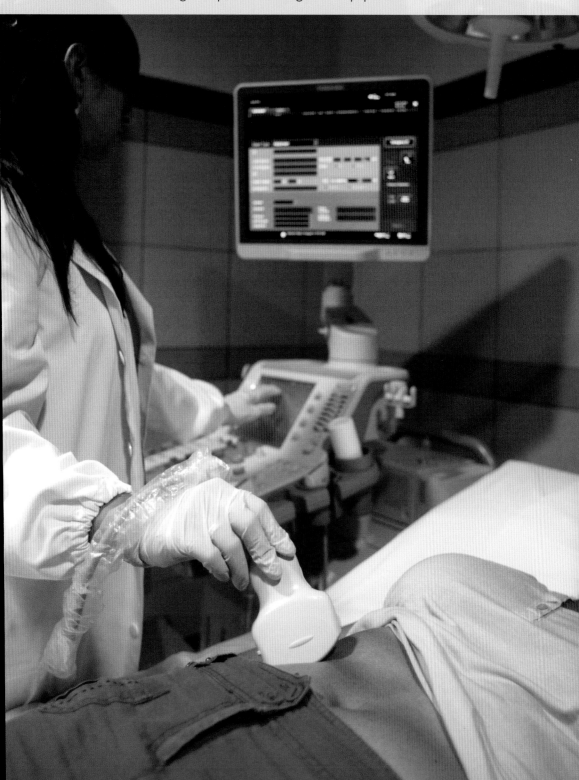

company. "For my current job, every time there is a software update, the FDA requires a set number of hours of testing. I test the software on several machines, and, if there is a problem, I write up an official report. Then I work with the engineers to solve the problem," she explains.

For most states, the entry-level requirement for a diagnostic medical technician is a two-year associate's degree or a postsecondary certificate. Many colleges and universities have programs for both associate's and bachelor's degrees in sonography. Nurses can even take a one-year program to obtain a certificate in the field. Some employers also require professional certification in addition to education. For high school students who are interested in pursuing a job as a diagnostic medical technician, it's recommended that they begin laying the groundwork by taking any courses offered at their school in anatomy, physiology, and mathematics.

Nuclear Medicine Technologists

Nuclear medicine technologists, just like diagnostic medical sonographers, use technology to create images of certain areas of the patient's body. Instead of using sonar technology to do this, however, the nuclear medicine technologist uses radioactive materials along with a special scanner to create the images. The purpose of the radioactive materials is to make abnormal areas of the body, such as tumors, appear distinct from the normal areas in the scanned image.

Nuclear medicine technologists typically just need an associate's degree in nuclear medicine technology, although a bachelor's degree in the same field is also an option. Some nuclear medicine technologists in the field today, like Colee Altom, received a bachelor's degree in a related field and then took additional courses for approximately one year to obtain a certificate in nuclear medical technology. "My undergraduate degree was in exercise science, and I wanted to continue along the same lines. Nuclear medicine requires that you take classes such as anatomy and physiology, physics, biology, college math, and a few other courses. I had already completed these courses as part of my undergraduate degree. . . So, my whole nuclear medicine school took only a year and a half. It was perfect!" In addition to the coursework, most states also require graduates of nuclear medicine programs to pass a licensure test in order to be employed in the state.

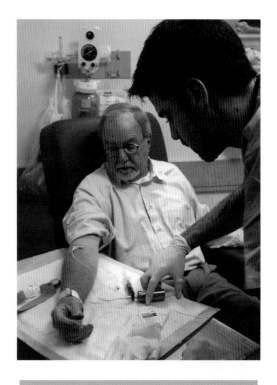

A nuclear medicine technologist preps a patient for a scan by giving him a dosage of F-18 FDG (a radioactive sugar analog), which helps with the imaging of tumors.

IN THE FIELD: MRI TECHNOLOGIST JOHN BLANCHARD

Why did you decide to become an MRI technologist?

MRI is a great job for people interested in biology as well as technology. Along with it comes the satisfaction of helping people figure out what is making them sick without having to slice them open for a look!

What are the major responsibilities of your job?

The responsibilities of an MRI tech mainly involve capturing images of a patient's anatomy (head, spine, abdomen, etc.) and manipulating those images in a way that helps doctors zero in on an accurate diagnosis. I also screen patients for harmful electronic implants (pacemakers, cochlear implants, neurostimulators) or metallic artifacts (shrapnel in veterans or metal workers), as any of these are potentially fatal around the MRI magnet.

What is your typical workday like?

A typical day in a hospital-based MRI setting involves scanning patients on a scheduled outpatient basis, while fitting in patients who need scans from the ER, as well as inpatients on the hospital floors. An MRI tech needs to use good judgment in who gets scanned first to last (a patient with a stroke before a patient with ankle pain, for instance) and have a solid plan on getting work completed in a way that keeps doctors informed and happy.

What are the pros and cons of your job?

Pros: I feel satisfaction in helping people with their health issues without resorting to invasive means (such as explorative surgery). I really enjoy slicing people up (virtually!) and looking to see what lies beneath their skin, to see what makes their bodies tick, and, if there is a prevailing problem, what can be done to remedy that. Technology in MRI is constantly changing, and there is always something new to learn and explore.

Cons: It's hard dealing with claustrophobic patients. Being shoved into a giant magnetic tube isn't always fun for everyone. Inpatients and older patients with age-related illnesses are also often difficult to work with. A patient who is having stroke symptoms is often confused and unaware of his or her surroundings and needs to be restrained in order to reduce motion for clear images.

Radiologic Technologists: MRIs, X-Rays, CT Scans

If you were to injure your leg while playing baseball, a radiologic technologist who specializes in administering X-ray images would help the doctor determine if your bone was broken. The X-ray technician would first prepare you for the imaging by finding out if there is any reason why you shouldn't have an X-ray. Once you have been properly screened and cleared, the technician would use the X-ray machine to take the image of your

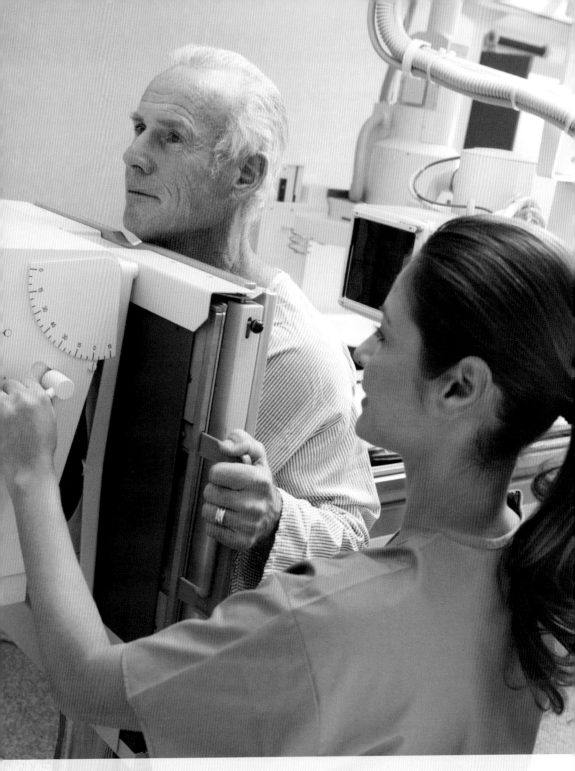

X-ray technicians help doctors see possible problems with a patient's skeletal system.

leg. Then, the X-ray technician would give the images to your doctor for him or her to examine and make the prognosis.

Radiologic technologists often start out as X-ray technicians. Then, with further training and education, they can become licensed to take other types of images like MRIs (magnetic resonance imaging) and CT scans (computed technology). In addition to finding out if bones are broken, these technologists also use their computerized equipment to find out if someone has had a stroke, has developed a cancerous tumor, or has abnormalities with internal organs.

Formal training programs vary. "I have an associate's degree," says radiologic technologist Kent Curtis. "There is also a limited X-ray technician certificate, which is a one-year program, but you can only work in a doctor's office with this." In an associate's degree program, a person takes such coursework as anatomy, pathology, patient care, radiation physics and protection, and image evaluation. Then the person completes a set number of hours of clinical work and passes a certification examination required by his or her state.

EKG/EEG/END Technologists

When someone is in the hospital, the patient is most often connected to a machine that shows his or her heart rate pattern. This machine is an electrocardiogram (EKG), and it shows the electrical activity of the heart. EKGs are often used to determine the cause of chest pain, to see how well medicines are working, to find out if implanted mechanical devices (such as pacemakers) are functioning properly, and to determine if heart walls are too thick.

WHERE WILL I WORK?

Job	Work Environment
Diagnostic medical sonographer	Hospitals, clinics, doctors' offices, labs
Nuclear medicine technologist	Hospitals, doctors' offices, labs, outpatient centers
Radiologic technologist	Hospitals, doctors' offices, labs, outpatient centers, federal government
EKG/EEG/END technologist	Hospitals, clinics, outpatient centers
Radiation therapist	Hospitals and cancer treatment centers
Respiratory therapist	Hospitals, nursing care facilities, patients' homes
Cardiovascular technologist	Hospitals, doctors' offices, labs, outpatient centers
Medical equipment preparer	Hospitals, doctors' offices, labs, outpatient centers
Medical equipment repairer	Professional and commercial equipment merchant wholesalers, hospitals, doctors' offices, labs, outpatient centers
Clinical research assistant	Hospitals, clinics, labs
Clinical research coordinator	Hospitals, clinics, labs
Dispensing optician	Doctors' offices, retail stores, department stores
Ophthalmology lab technician	Optometry labs
Ophthalmology technician	Doctors' offices
Occupational health and safety technician	State and local government, hospitals, mining and other industries, waste management, consulting services

Occupational health and safety specialist	State and local government, hospitals, mining and other industries, waste management, consulting services
Dental assistant	Dentists' offices
Dental hygienist	Dentists' offices
Dental laboratory technician	Dental laboratories
Medical appliance technician	Prosthetist offices or prosthetist labs
Veterinary technician	Veterinary offices, clinics, or animal hospitals

While an EKG shows the electrical activity of the heart, an EEG (electroencephalogram) shows the electrical activity of the brain. EEGs help physicians determine why a patient is experiencing seizures or confusion. They can show whether a head injury has caused permanent damage. They also reveal other problems in the brain like tumors, infections, and diseases like Alzheimer's.

An END (electroneurodiagnostic) test reveals if there are any problems with the electrical activity of the central and peripheral nervous systems. The information obtained from this test can be used by physicians to diagnose strokes and seizures. It also helps them determine how best to treat headaches, dizziness, and degenerative brain diseases and determine their root causes.

Technologists who monitor these machines are required to have completed training in a certification program or have obtained an associate's degree. Once the coursework is complete, the technologist must also finish a specific number of hours of clinical work with patients and then take an oral and written examination for certification.

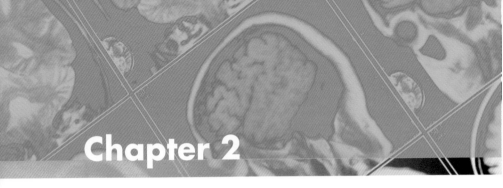

Chapter 2

Using Technology to Treat Illness

Technology has greatly improved our ability to diagnose illness and disease. It has also vastly expanded the arsenal of weapons we can use to treat disease and cure illness. Being a part of the cutting-edge solution to a health problem—on a daily basis—is thrilling and enormously gratifying.

Radiation Therapists

A radiation therapist is part of an oncology team that treats cancer patients. Other people on the team include radiation oncologists, oncology nurses, radiation physicists, and medical dosimetrists. The oncologist determines what treatment is needed. Then, the medical dosimetrist calculates the correct dosage. Once the dosage has been determined, the patient visits the radiation therapist to receive the treatment.

When the patient arrives at the radiation clinic or hospital, the radiation therapist visits with the patient to explain the treatment and answer any questions. Then, the therapist administers the treatment after having looked

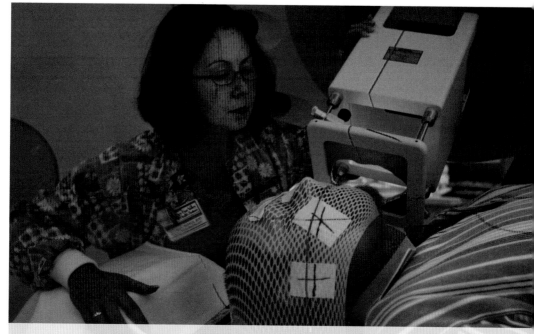

Radiation therapists use specialized machines (this one uses lasers) to administer radiation to patients with cancer. Advancements in this technology continue to save more lives every year.

over an X-ray to make sure it's being administered to the correct location. Following the procedure, the therapist makes sure the patient does not have any adverse or unusual reactions. In addition to administering the treatment, the radiation therapist is also responsible for making sure the equipment is working properly. He or she must keep detailed records of every procedure.

Formal education is required for this job. Most college or university programs lead to either an associate's degree or a bachelor's degree. Some certificate programs can be finished in only twelve months. However, it may be more difficult to find a job with only this much training since most employers do prefer a degree over a certificate. Most states also require a license, which can be obtained by passing a certification exam.

Respiratory Therapists

People of all ages (premature infants to the elderly) who have trouble breathing are often helped by a respiratory therapist. This health care professional provides emergency respiratory care to people suffering heart attacks, strokes, near-drowning, or shock. Respiratory therapists also offer continuing care for people with asthma, chronic respiratory disease, and emphysema.

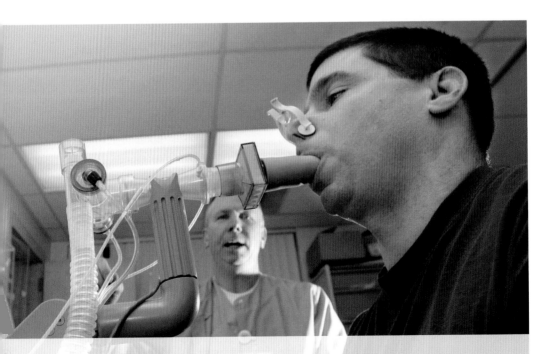

Respiratory therapists work in many settings and with many different types of patients. This therapist is working with a firefighter to test his lung capacity. Some firehouses throughout the country are taking preventative measures to help their firefighters achieve and maintain better overall health.

Respiratory therapists test a patient's breathing by using equipment that measures the volume and flow of oxygen when inhaled and exhaled. They take blood samples to find out the oxygen level of the blood. They might also help patients remove mucus from their lungs by applying various methods. When patients are having serious breathing problems, therapists will connect the patients to a ventilator.

Respiratory therapists must have an associate's degree and a state license in order to be employed in the field. Oftentimes, further education (a bachelor's degree) will help a person find work more easily. Coursework includes microbiology, anatomy, physiology, physics, chemistry, pharmacology, and mathematics. High school students interested in this field are encouraged to take similar courses to prepare themselves for their college coursework.

Cardiovascular Technologists

Cardiovascular technologists work directly with a heart doctor (cardiologist) to perform procedures on a patient. These procedures can be both invasive and noninvasive. The invasive procedures include cardiac catheterization, while the noninvasive procedures include EKG, vascular ultrasound, and electrophysiology. The physician will then use the information obtained in these procedures to make the diagnosis of the patient's cardiovascular condi-tion (the state and relative health of his or her heart and circulatory system).

Cardiovascular technologists generally have an associ-ate's degree, although some have more education (bachelor's degree) and others have less (on-the-job

IN THE FIELD: EKG TECHNICIAN AUNDREA GRIFFITH

What training did you need for your job?
The type of training depends on where you work. My hospital required that I take a two-hour class that was held once a week for twelve weeks. After the class was finished, I had to take a test and pass it with 80 percent accuracy. Most people have to take this test more than once to pass. I know a few people who have taken it three to four times and haven't passed it yet.

What is your typical workday like?
Each day, I "run a strip" every four hours. This means that I diagnose one six-second strip per patient on the monitors every day. I will also watch up to forty-eight monitors at a time. The system is set up to a computer with three different screens, and each one has sixteen patients per monitor. The system is programmed to beep when it thinks there is something wrong. Yet, the computers do not always pick up the little things. That is my job. I am trained to see the little changes in a patient's heart rhythm before it becomes a big problem. Throughout my shift, I have to answer phones and call lights and also keep track of where the patients are when they aren't in their room. I stay in constant communication with the nurses to alert them to problems with their patients. Because of the size of my unit, that means I have to stay in contact with about eighteen different people. And that is not counting all of the doctors and therapists. Most of the doctors will come up and ask me questions about their patients, so I

have to know exactly what is going on because they don't like to wait for me to figure it out. The patients' families also come to the desk to ask questions. It can be very stressful at times. The worst is when I have more than one patient coding at the same time.

What are the pros and cons of your job?

The truth is, with my job, the good would not be there without the bad. I love my job because at any time I could be a person who helps save someone's life. That is definitely a positive aspect of my job. In contrast, there are some people whom, no matter what you do, you can't save them. It is really hard when someone dies, especially when you're not expecting it. I have seen patients on more than one occasion who look great on the monitors for days, and then, all of a sudden, they are in a situation that, no matter what we do, we cannot save them. One of the other things I like about my job is that, because of the type of patients we take care of, we see some of them a lot. So you get to know them and their families, and they often become friends.

What advice do you have for teens interested in this job?

The advice that I would give to teenagers is that no matter what job they get in the medical field—whether it be a tech or a doctor—they have to want to help people. If they don't want to do that, they will not like this job. Also it is not like you see on television. No hospital is like *Gray's Anatomy*. So don't go in expecting that or you will be disappointed.

training). Lauren Jaworowski is currently a student in a registered cardiovascular invasive specialist program. She has a bachelor's of science in biology and decided to continue her education by obtaining an additional degree. "I attend classes as well as clinicals, which involve watching and helping with cardiac catheterization procedures three days per week. I can help monitor, circulate, or scrub in on the catheterization," she explains. "I really like learning about all of the new technology in the field. It is amazing what they can do with catheters and an X-ray machine. I also enjoy helping out in the labs and feeling like a part of the team."

Medical Equipment Preparers

Immediately after high school graduation, a person can obtain a job as a medical equipment preparer. For this job, little or no post–high school education is required. In fact, most people receive on-the-job training. However, if a person wants to advance in this field, some kind of formal education—such as an associate's degree—is necessary. This job is also known as a sterile supply technician.

As a medical equipment preparer, a person's main responsibility is to use disinfecting solutions to sterilize laboratory and health care equipment such as respirators, wheelchairs, hospital beds, and oxygen and dialysis machines. In addition to using chemical solutions, the person may also use equipment such as autoclaves in the sterilization process. These responsibilities are extremely important since the presence of disease-causing microorganisms on hospital equipment can be very dangerous for both the patients and the hospital staff. In addition to sanitizing equipment, a person employed in this job also prepares, installs, and maintains equipment. Medical equipment preparers can do all of these tasks in hospitals, clinics, laboratories, or even at a patient's home.

Medical Equipment Repairers

Medical equipment repairers test, adjust, and repair biomedical or electromedical equipment. Gary Jones is a field service representative for a biomedical service company today, but he started out his career as a biomedical technician in a hospital setting. He works out of his home office and travels to clinics, medical offices, and laboratories to repair equipment, perform updates, and conduct preventative maintenance. "My job is not an 8 AM to 5 PM position, although it could be. Some days, I work four hours; other days, I work ten hours. It's all dependent on what work I have to complete and what customer issues I may have. It all balances out, though, in the end," he explains.

A person in this field must have expertise and knowledge in any or all of the following: computers and electronics, engineering and technology, mathematics, and mechanics. At the very least, this job requires an associate's degree in biomedical technology or engineering. There are also some opportunities to do apprentice work in this field, specifically as an electromedical-equipment repairer, a dental-equipment installer and servicer, or a biomedical equipment technician.

To get his degree, Gary Jones took night classes at a technical school. He didn't feel there was much chance for advancement in the hospital setting, so he decided to try out fieldwork. "With my current company, I can advance up the ranks to specialist, service support, and management," he explains.

Clinical Research Assistants and Clinical Research Coordinators

A clinical research assistant spends his or her day working in a laboratory or health care facility and collecting samples from people. He or she then runs basic lab tests on the samples, including drug screenings, pregnancy

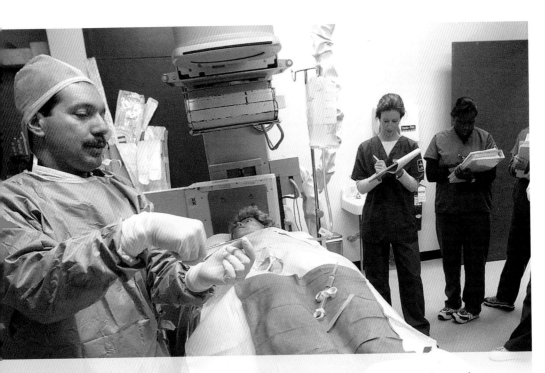

Students in the medical technology field are trained through coursework, live demonstrations, and hands-on lab work.

tests, and other vital tests. The results of these tests can also be used as part of an official study conducted by a pharmaceutical company. The assistant's other duties include gathering paperwork and signatures and entering them in the proper databases.

Brittany Jones started out in the animal care industry. She then decided to make a career change and obtained a job as a clinical research assistant at a pharmaceutical company. "I had a strong desire to help people and started looking for jobs that would allow me to use my medical knowledge and fulfill my drive to help out." There isn't a specified degree that is necessary for this job, but as Jones suggests, "A degree in a related field or general knowledge of biology, chemistry, pharmaceuticals, or psychology is certainly helpful."

Jones worked as an assistant for a number of years. She took advantage of an opportunity to advance in the industry when a position for a clinical research coordinator became available. A coordinator oversees the clinical research assistants, performs many other managerial tasks, and works directly with the doctors and nurses in the clinical studies. She was able to secure this position by learning all aspects of clinical research and demonstrating her ability and experience in the field.

Chapter 3

Technology Jobs Outside a Hospital Setting

Medical technology jobs are not limited to those found in hospitals, labs, and clinics. There are also many opportunities to work in the field in other professional settings , including dentists' offices, veterinarians' offices, ophthalmology offices, and prosthetic offices. Professionals who ensure the safety of construction sites and industrial workplaces are also part of the field of medical technology.

Dispensing Opticians

Anyone who wears glasses has probably used the services of a dispensing optician. This is the person who helps fit a patient with eyeglasses or contacts. Usually, after a patient meets with an eye doctor and it's determined that eyeglasses are necessary, the patient next meets with the dispensing optician.

The dispensing optician shows the patient all of the frames available and gives suggestions as to which ones look best with his or her face shape. The optician will also discuss lens options with the patient, including those that are tinted (or will automatically tint in bright light) and nonreflective lenses, as well as single vision, bifocal, trifocal, or progressive lenses. In addition to this responsibility, dispensing opticians adjust frames when the patient comes to pick up the glasses. They repair frames if and when the patient damages them. The dispensing optician also takes care of general paperwork and handles insurance claims.

Dispensing opticians often work in an eye doctor's office or in a retail or department store that sells eyeglasses. This job doesn't necessarily require any advance training. A high school diploma is ordinarily sufficient to

Dispensing opticians help people look great in their new eyeglasses and insure a proper fit that will optimize both comfort and vision.

get hired, and then the person is trained on the job. Some states require certification, and others do not. In the ophthalmology field, many other technologist jobs are also available, including ophthalmology lab technicians and ophthalmology technicians.

Ophthalmology Lab Technicians

After a person orders a pair of prescription glasses or contacts from a dispensing optician, the order then goes to a laboratory where an ophthalmology lab technician fulfills the order. This job requires a high school diploma and little or no post-secondary education. Most professional training is completed on the job.

Some medical technicians, like ophthalmology lab technicians, have little to no interaction with the public. This is good news for people who would rather work behind the scenes.

Ophthalmology lab technicians are also known as manufacturing opticians, optical mechanics, and optical goods workers. They can work in an actual laboratory at a manufacturing supplies company or they can work inside the office of either an ophthalmologist or optometrist. People in these jobs have very little, if any, contact with the public. They just work behind the scenes cutting and shaping lenses, dipping lenses into coatings (for tinting and nonreflective orders), polishing lenses, assembling the lenses into the frames, and then inspecting the final product. In addition to making lenses for eyeglasses, people in this job can also make lenses for other medical, scientific, and recreational equipment including telescopes, microscopes, and binoculars.

Occupational Health and Safety Technicians and Specialists

Back in the late 1800s in the United States, the workplace was often quite dangerous. Many people lost limbs, eyesight, hearing, and even their lives because of long hours on the job and unsafe machines, practices, and environments. Because of legislation pushed by progressives in the early 1900s, however, workers now have more assurances that they will remain safe on the job and receive just compensation if they are hurt or disabled at work. Accidents still happen, of course, but at least there are systems set up to better help protect workers and ensure their welfare and health care if disabled (permanently or temporarily) on the job.

One way that workplaces are made safer today is through the inspections of occupational health and safety

IN THE FIELD:
VETERINARY TECHNICIAN
KAYLENE JACOBSEN

Where can a veterinary technician work?

As a technician, you can get a job in a hospital for larger animals, like livestock and farm animals, or a vet clinic for smaller animals, like cats, dogs, birds, rodents, and reptiles. You can work at labs that deal with samples that vet clinics send out. You can also work at a zoo.

What training did you need for your job?

In most states, you need to be certified to be a veterinary technician. In other states (like the one I live in), it is not required to be certified. Some technical schools and colleges offer programs for veterinary assistants and technicians. I took classes while I was still in high school through a local technical school. For part of my certification, I had to complete a certain amount of hours as an intern at a veterinary clinic.

What is your typical workday like?

Every clinic, or hospital, is different. Since I work at a pet hospital, the techs all have different job duties. We have room technicians and surgical technicians. There are usually three room technicians and three surgery technicians at the hospital every day. Room technicians get the patients in for their appointments and help the doctors during the appointments. They also help take care of the animals that have had overnight surgeries or are being boarded at the hospital. Surgical technicians help the doctor who is doing surgery that day. They intake all patients, draw up the drugs, prepare the animals for surgery, and monitor them afterward while they are recovering from anesthesia.

What advice do you have for teens who are interested in this job?

My advice would be to really look into the job first. Like any career, it's not all fun and games. A lot of people just assume that we get to play with puppies and kittens all day. But that is not the case. My other advice would be to go school and get formally educated as a veterinary technician, even if your state does not require that. The knowledge that you gain will help with getting a job and also in the workplace.

technicians and specialists. Technicians perform a variety of tasks to find out if the workplace is safe for employees. They collect samples of toxic (or potentially toxic) materials such as chemicals, dust, molds, gases, and vapors. They then give these samples to the specialists for analysis. The technicians also inspect the overall workplace. They closely examine the equipment (scaffolding, forklifts, etc.) and practices of the workers (hardhat and mask usage, etc.) to make sure that all are in compliance with the government's safety standards and regulations.

Most occupational health and safety technicians are trained on the job, yet some also obtain their employment after they have obtained an associate's degree or certificate. Specialists generally need a bachelor's degree.

Dental Assistants and Dental Hygienists

When Ciera Brown was a senior in high school, she started taking classes at a local technical college. "I had to do both coursework and clinical work," she explains. "Then, I had to complete three hundred hours for my internship. It was great, though, because when I graduated from high school, I also graduated from the technical college with my degree as a dental assistant."

Programs vary by state for dental assisting. Some require graduation from an accredited program (which usually takes about one year), while others allow on-the-job training. Dental assistants perform a variety of tasks. They sterilize instruments, process X-rays, keep records of dental treatments, schedule appointments, work with patients on billing, help make

If they plan properly, dental assistants, like Ciera Brown (shown here), can obtain their certificates at the same time as high school graduation.

patients comfortable before and during treatment, and help the dentist during procedures.

Dental hygienists must complete an associate's degree and obtain a certificate in dental hygiene. Coursework generally includes anatomy, nutrition, physiology, periodontology, radiography, and gum disease. Entrance into dental hygiene programs can be quite competitive. "Depending on the school, some have waiting periods of two to five years once you meet the requirements, and others simply take the highest qualified applicants based on grades, experience, and interviews," explains dental hygienist Amber Ellis.

Dental hygienists must have specific capabilities and skills. They must have the ability to show compassion to patients who are distressed. They must be detail-oriented, have manual dexterity and physical stamina for repetitive tasks, and exhibit technical skills in order to operate the machines and tools used in the industry.

Dental Laboratory Technicians

So, let's say you go to the dentist and find out that you need to get a crown on one of your molars. Who makes this artificial tooth? The answer is a dental laboratory technician. These technicians don't just make crowns, though. They also make other dental prosthetics and devices such as bridges, veneers, dentures, teeth for dental implants, and retainers. Dental laboratory technicians work with a variety of tools (files, polishers, etc.) and materials (porcelain, wax, plastic, plaster, and pastes).

Most dental laboratory technicians come into the workforce with just a high school diploma and learn their skills on the job. However, some do obtain an associate's degree at a technical college.

Medical Appliance Technicians

A prosthetist is a professional with at least a master's degree who fits patients with artificial limbs and braces. A medical appliance technician helps the prosthetist with basic responsibilities in the office. Technicians might be asked to create a mold or pattern for the prosthetic. Technicians could also be asked to assist prosthetists by handing them the power tools while the device is being made. Technicians may help fit patients with the devices once they're finished. They can also repair the devices if they've been damaged during use.

Medical appliance technicians generally do not need any specific education following high school graduation. They will be trained on the job. High school courses that could prove helpful for this job include mathematics, science, metal and wood shop, and computers.

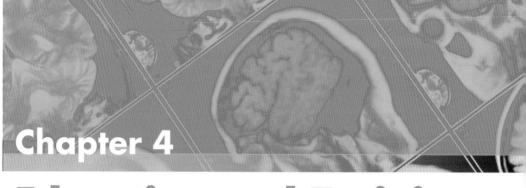

Chapter 4

Education and Training for a Career in Medical Technology

For the various medical technology careers featured in this book, the amount of education and training varies. With some jobs, a person needs only a high school diploma and can be trained on the job. Other jobs require a one-year certificate or a two-year associate's degree. Very few require a four-year bachelor's degree, and most of these are jobs that medical technology professionals would advance to after they've been in the field for a while.

The fact that so little education is required for most of these jobs gives a great amount of hope to teens who would like to break into the medical field shortly after they graduate from high school. Many of these medical technology positions also pay very well. In fact, the pay rate of these positions would be very difficult to duplicate in other fields with the same amount of education and training. To find out more about the current median pay for your field of interest, visit the United States Department of Labor's Bureau of Labor Statistics' online *Occupational Outlook Handbook*.

IN THE FIELD: DENTAL HYGIENIST AMBER ELLIS

What are the major responsibilities of your job?

Basically, a hygienist's job is all about making sure people have healthy mouths. This includes diagnosing gum disease, deciding what type of oral health care needs each patient requires based upon their individual situation, cleaning teeth and gums, and then teaching people how to take care of their teeth and gums. I often tell people that the dentist takes care of their teeth, and I help them take care of everything that holds their teeth in place: the gums and the bone. The healthiest, prettiest teeth in the world are no good if they fall out because someone didn't take care of their gums!

What is your typical workday like?

I arrive at work about twenty minutes before the first scheduled patient to set up for the day. I review the records of the patients who are scheduled for the day, including any specific medical issues or other potential difficulties. I meet for about five minutes with all the office staff to make sure the day will run smoothly and we'll have the fewest complications possible. I see about two patients per hour until lunch. Then, I take a one-hour lunch, then back to work again until the office closes around 5 PM. I seldom stay beyond 5 PM. In our office, we see all ages from about 2 ½ years old to 98 years old. So, in one day, we have a good mix of people.

What are the pros and cons of your job?

Pros: I have great hours. I never work on major holidays, weekends, or evenings. I especially love it that I don't take work home with me. Many hygienists work part-time so they can take care of a family, and they can pretty much say how many or how few hours they would like to work. The wages are quite good, but will vary greatly depending on where you live.

Cons: The work is very repetitive. Yet this doesn't bother me too much because I find variety in the people I talk to and help. I have a lot of people tell me that they couldn't stand to work in other people's mouths because of spit, blood, or bad smells. That doesn't bother me, but I guess that could also be a con to some people.

Getting trained and hired as a dental hygienist is a rigorous process. But those who make it through, like Amber Ellis (shown here), definitely appreciate the job for all of its benefits, including good pay, great hours, and a rewarding working environment.

Getting Started While Still in High School

Even though further education is not necessarily required after graduation, there are things that teens can do during high school to prepare for these jobs. "Start taking classes in high school, such as anatomy, physiology, chemistry, and biology," advises radiologic technologist Kent Curtis.

In addition, MRI technologist John Blanchard suggests, "Work hard in your classes. Good grades and a well-prepared student interview can save years of time waiting for acceptance into a program," he explains. "That's because some colleges accept students into their programs based on a waitlist, while others evaluate

Taking advanced science courses while still in high school will definitely give prospective medical technologists a leg-up over their competition.

candidates strictly off of their prerequisite courses and student interviews. Exceptionally good grades in college prerequisites such as math, English, anatomy, and physiology will give you an edge over other applicants."

Technical Schools, Community Colleges, and Online Learning

Some medical technology jobs require education that can often be obtained at technical schools, community colleges, and universities.

If you're interested in pursuing a job in medical technology, you should start looking at programs during your senior year of high school. Many trade or technical schools offer courses in the medical technology field. So do community colleges. Visit colleges in person or on the Internet to find out about specific programs. Make sure the school is accredited. This means that the curriculum is recognized by a national board and is therefore sufficient for licensure and certification. Ask other students who have attended the school about their experience. Did they have a positive or negative

What Education or Training Will I Need?

Job	On-the-job training?	Short-term, 1-year, or associate's degree?	Advanced education (additional certificates or bachelor's degree) available?	Must I take continuing education to keep my certificate valid?
Diagnostic medical sonographer	NO	YES	YES, but not required	YES
Nuclear medicine technologist	NO	YES	YES, but not required	YES
Radiologic technologist	NO	YES	YES, but not required	YES
EKG/EEG/END technologist	NO	YES	YES, but not required	YES
Radiation therapist	NO	YES	YES	YES
Respiratory therapist	NO	YES	YES, but not required	YES
Cardiovascular technologist	YES	YES	YES, but not required	YES
Medical equipment preparer	YES	YES	NO	YES, on the job
Medical equipment repairer	NO	YES	YES	YES
Clinical research assistant	YES	NO	NO	YES
Clinical research coordinator	YES	NO	NO	YES
Dispensing optician	YES	NO	NO	YES
Ophthalmology lab technician	YES	NO	NO	Yes, on the job

Ophthalmology technician	YES	YES	NO	YES
Occupational health and safety technician	YES	YES	YES	Certification not required, but encouraged
Occupational health and safety specialist	NO	NO	YES	YES
Dental assistant	YES, but not in all states	YES	NO	YES
Dental hygienist	NO	YES	YES	YES
Dental laboratory technicians	YES	NO	NO	YES, often on the job
Medical appliance technician	YES	NO	NO	YES, often on the job
Veterinary technician	YES, but not common	YES	YES	YES

one, and why? If you don't personally know anyone who has attended the school, you could find alumni online by using a search engine or by networking on social media sites.

You don't necessarily have to take classes on campus since many colleges offer courses online. Distance-education courses were particularly helpful to ophthalmology technician Hannah Anderson. "I cross-trained with the other technicians in our office at first," she explains. "To become certified, though, I took an online course. It was easier to do this because it was at my own pace versus being in a classroom setting."

People interested in medical technology careers should follow a professional in the field on his or her job. This job shadowing experience will give prospective technologists an idea of whether or not they even like the job.

Job Shadowing

Prior to starting any coursework either online or in a class-room, there's one very important thing that a student really must do—job shadow. Every professional medical technologist who was interviewed for this book agreed that this was his or her number one advice for teens who are interested in the industry. After all, you don't want to choose a job, go through all of the education and training, and then find out that you really don't even like this type of work. That's definitely a huge waste of time and money. So, find someone in the field, and ask if you can follow him or her around for a day or two to see what the job is really like. If you don't know someone personally, you can contact a specific place of work (hospital, doctor's office, laboratory, etc.) or official organization (such as a national accreditation board) and ask whom you could talk to about setting something like that up.

Diagnostic sonographer Wendy Reynolds suggests that when a person job shadows he or she should "ask lots of questions and really try to job shadow in several different places. The reason for this is because a hospital environment is a lot different to work in than an outpatient clinic. And working on the business side, as I do in an ultrasound manufacturing company, is a very different experience than working in patient care."

Chapter 5

Hunting for a Job

O nce you've finished your education, you'll need to start looking for a job. Some of the professionals in the field argue, however, that your job search should actually start before you finish your training, not after. MRI technologist John Blanchard advises, "Keep your ear to the ground during training. Ask experienced techs where the jobs are and seek out opportunities to help out in other departments. In other words, it's essential to market and promote yourself from the ground floor up."

Principle radiologic technologist Carla Leon Guerrero agrees. "The most important thing is to show your interest and make a great impression on your future employers during training because if you don't, they won't remember you."

Treat the Job Hunt as a Full-Time Job

The same amount of effort that goes into finding a training program for your career should also go into finding a job. Attend job fairs. Visit government-sponsored job help centers, employment offices, and even temporary

Give a smile and a firm handshake when you meet your interviewer. Never call him or her by a first name unless directed to do so.

employment ("temp") agencies. Spend time online looking at job boards. Promote yourself on such professional social networking sites as LinkedIn and Twitter. Join professional online message boards for your particular field and actively respond to posts. Make connections with other people in the industry and ask them if they know of any available jobs. If you don't have access to the Internet at home or on your phone, you can visit a public library to conduct your searches for free.

As you're actively engaged in the job search, you should also be preparing yourself for future interviews. The first thing you should do is compose a neat and organized résumé and print it on professional paper. At

IN THE FIELD: RADIATION THERAPIST CHRIS DAVIS

What are the major responsibilities of your job?

As a radiation therapist, my major responsibilities are to perform the daily radiation therapy treatments that are prescribed by the radiation oncologist. These patients are undergoing radiation treatments for cancer. They come daily for their appointments, and I position the patient by the machine, set the machine to the correct settings and dose, and execute the treatment. Patient care and exactness in following the treatment plan is of utmost importance.

Was it difficult to find a job after you finished your education?

No, I was able to work for the same radiation oncology practice that I did my clinical rotation with. They allowed me to do my student training at the clinic and then hired me after I finished my training.

What are the pros and cons of your job?

There are many benefits of working as a radiation therapist. I always seem to work with very grateful patients who appreciate my attention to detail and kind demeanor. The difficult part of working in this field is that some patients are not able to complete their treatment due to the nature of the disease. It's easy to develop strong attachments to people whom you see almost every day, and it's hard to know that they won't be coming back.

Do you have to work long hours at your job?
Radiation therapy is generally delivered Monday through Friday, from 8 AM to 5 PM. Yet, some facilities start earlier and some stay open later. There generally is not any weekend or afterhours work to be done.

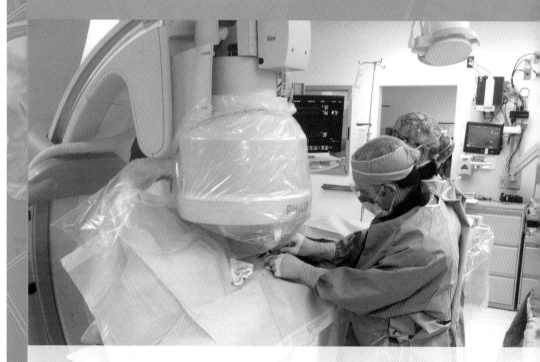

Chris Davis's daily routine as a radiation therapist includes working on patients who are undergoing cancer treatment. As shown here, he works alongside other medical technologists with state-of-the-art equipment that uses cutting-edge technology.

this early stage of your career, a one-sided résumé is sufficient. Include only the most pertinent information, and always be honest with what you include. Never make up things or "pad" your résumé to make it more attractive to employers. In the end, the truth will always be revealed, and you will tarnish your reputation and possibly eliminate career opportunities if you choose to be dishonest about your education or experience.

Of course, the ultimate goal in the job search is to get an interview. This might take a great deal of time, or it might happen almost immediately. This depends on many factors: how many job searchers there are in relation to the number of jobs; how willing you are to relocate to a different geographic area; how much demand there is for your specific job skills; and how qualified you are in comparison to other candidates.

When that happy day arrives and you finally get called for an interview, you'll want to be prepared. Here are some tips to follow before, during, and after an interview.

Before the Interview

- Practice with a friend on how you'll answer questions about yourself and your qualifications.
- Do some preliminary research on the company and make up a list of questions that you'd like to ask about both the company and the job.
- On the day of the interview, shower, apply deodorant, do your hair, brush your teeth, and use mouthwash.

- Wear proper clothing. Business professional is always the best option—suit and tie for men, suit with skirt or pants for women.
- Print several copies of your résumé and references on professional-quality paper and bring them with you to the interview.

During the Interview

- Smile and shake hands firmly with the interviewer. Refer to him or her as "Mr. or Ms. [Last Name]" unless instructed to do otherwise.

Medical technologists often wear scrubs on the job. However, that type of attire would be highly inappropriate for an interview. Business professional attire is always the best bet.

THE DOS AND DON'TS OF USING SOCIAL MEDIA FOR JOB SEARCHING

Dos	Don'ts
✓ Make your Facebook account private, so only your friends can see your posts and photos. Or take the time to set up an area specifically for professional contacts and limit what they are able to see.	✓ Don't post inappropriate status updates or pictures of yourself (partying, etc.) that could hinder your chances of finding a job should a future employer see them.
✓ Post on your social media account the type of job that you're trying to find and ask others if they know of any opportunities.	✓ Don't have inconsistencies in your online work profile versus your printed resume. Make sure they're both the same. Otherwise, the inconsistencies may make prospective employers think you are lying about your résumé, experience, and qualifications.
✓ Include your Twitter handle and LinkedIn profile on your résumé.	
✓ Join conversations in your industry on Twitter and LinkedIn and actively participate in them.	✓ Don't update your accounts (Twitter, for example) so much that you become obnoxious. Update just enough to keep your presence active.
✓ Start networking with hiring managers and other people in the business on Twitter and LinkedIn.	✓ Don't brag about yourself when you share your accomplishments.

✓ Keep your LinkedIn account active so that it will pop up first on a Google search of your name.	✓ Don't share too much information about your personal life.
✓ Network, network, network! Make connections in your industry, the earlier, the better. Be willing to help others in their job search, too. After all, networking works both ways.	✓ Don't forget to proofread your postings to ensure you haven't made grammatical or other errors, especially on Twitter. These posts are forever and can't be deleted or edited later on.
✓ Share your accomplishments on your social media accounts.	✓ Don't forget that everyone has a different sense of humor. Don't post things that may be offensive to others, especially prospective employers.

- Do not slouch. Sit up straight and look the interviewer in the eye during the conversation.
- Do not chew gum, candy, mints, or anything similarly distracting.
- Answer each question concisely. Use proper English when you speak and avoid slang.
- Ask specific, detailed, and knowledgeable questions about the position, the company, the workplace, and what your responsibilities would be. This shows that you have taken the initiative to do research beforehand.
- Ask the interviewer for his or her business card. This will give you the information you need for follow-up correspondence.

After the Interview

- Within a day of the interview, write and mail a thank-you note to the interviewer. E-mail is also an option but is less personal.
- Spend some time analyzing the interview. Give yourself honest feedback on how you could have improved and also the things you did well.

Looking for a job should be a full-time job. One health care professional notes, "You are not actually actively looking for a job unless you have fifty résumés out at one time." Now, this number may not be possible to attain, but the principle behind the idea is a good one. Get out there and search every day in every way you can. Fill out applications. Send out résumés. Network with friends and family members, and ask them to let you know if they hear of a job in your field. Properly prepare for your interviews. If you are proactive about finding a job, eventually that hard work will pay off and you will be successful at securing one.

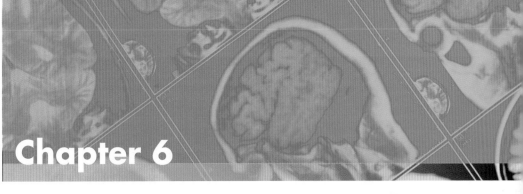

Chapter 6

Climbing the Health Care Ladder

Congratulations! Your efforts have finally paid off, and you have landed the medical technology job of your dreams. Now, fast forward a little in time. You've been working hard at your job for several years. You enjoy the people you work with and the tasks and responsibilities of the job. However, you're not the type of person who likes to sit still and become stagnant. You want to keep moving forward and climb the health care ladder. But how do you do that?

Explore Your Options

There are many opportunities in the medical technology field for advancement, in terms of job title, responsibilities, and pay scale. Just about all of the opportunities require additional training, be it on the job or in a classroom setting. Some opportunities are in new but related skill areas. A radiologic technologist, for example, can get further training and certification in ultrasound, nuclear medicine, special intervention procedures, MRI, and CT scans.

IN THE FIELD: OPHTHALMOLOGY TECHNICIAN HANNAH ANDERSON

Why did you decide to become an ophthalmology technician?

I started working as the receptionist and decided that I enjoyed learning about what was going on with the patients' eyes more than just checking them in for their appointments.

What are the major responsibilities of your job?

I work hands-on with our doctor in the exam rooms. He is an ophthalmologist. I input the exam information into the computer as he is dictating it to me. If I am not in the room with the doctor, I am preparing the patients for their appointment. That consists of taking their vision complaints, checking their vision, and inputting it all into the computer for the doctor to go over before he sees them.

What is your typical workday like?

A typical day at my job starts at 8:00 AM. I go into the office and open the rooms, start up the equipment and computers for the doctor, and print the day's schedule. While I'm doing this, the first patient gets prepped by my coworker, and then the doctor and I see the patient. I enter the exam information into the system as the doctor does the exam. I take the patient out to the checkout desk and issue his or her prescriptions, samples, or anything that he or she needs. When we are done with patients at the end of the day, I clean the rooms, shut the equipment down, and close the rooms.

Do you have to work long hours at your job?

Our office is mostly open weekdays, 8 AM to 5 AM. We do work different hours on some days just to make it easier for our patients.

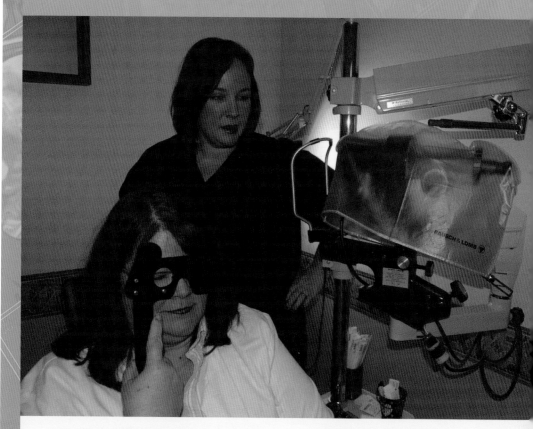

Hannah Anderson has a variety of responsibilities in her job as an ophthalmology technician. Here, she performs a vision test on a patient.

Other opportunities are in management. "In large hospitals, there are chief techs who are given more administrative responsibilities to ensure that workflow in a department is handled efficiently," explains MRI technologist John Blanchard. Still other opportunities can take medical technologists out of patient care altogether and into the business world. A student in a registered cardiovascular invasive specialist program, Lauren Jaworowski, explains that in her field, "Many companies that design the technologies for our industry often recruit techs to become reps for their companies."

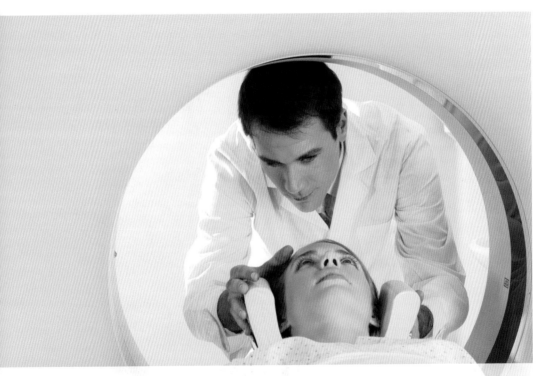

MRI technologists must sometimes work with patients who are claustrophobic (or afraid of being in tight enclosed spaces). Having a kind and caring demeanor with patients is of particular importance in these situations.

Just Do It!

It's important to realize that these opportunities aren't automatically available to everyone. If you want to climb the health care ladder, you must work hard to be an exceptional employee. You can't show up late to work, do a subpar job, be discourteous to patients and fellow employees, be disrespectful to your boss, and still expect to move forward in the workplace. That's just not going to happen. You must take your career seriously if you want to keep your job, let alone advance in the workplace. You want to be the type of employee that your company cannot live without.

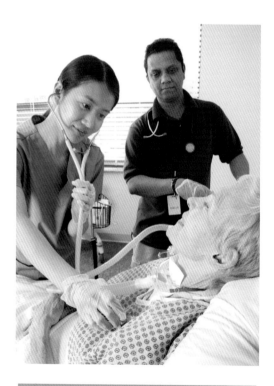

Medical technologists assist doctors and nurses as they treat patients in hospitals, clinics, and doctors' offices.

To identify advancement opportunities, you can use the same strategies employed to secure your job in the first place. You can search online, network with other colleagues, attend job fairs, read professional journals, and join professional organizations. You can

WILL I HAVE ANY OPPORTUNITIES FOR ADVANCEMENT?

Job	Opportunities for Advancement
Diagnostic medical sonographers	Can be trained to become radiologic technologists and nuclear medicine technologists.
Nuclear medicine technologists	Can be trained to become radiologic technologist and diagnostic sonographers.
Radiologic technologists	Radiologic technologists often start out as X-ray techs. They can then go on to get further training in MRI and CT scans. Later, they can further their training to become radiation therapists.
EKG/EEG/END technologists	EKG/EEG/END technologists can go back to school to get trained in any of the related fields (radiologic technologists, nuclear medicine technologists, diagnostic sonographers).
Radiation therapists	Radiation therapists can continue their education to become medical dosimetrists or even radiation oncologists, oncology nurses, or radiation physicists.
Respiratory therapists	Respiratory therapists can go back to school to become registered nurses or doctors.

Cardiovascular technologists	Cardiovascular technologists can go back to school to obtain a more advanced degree. This would allow them to have more opportunities and an increase in pay.
Medical equipment preparers	Preparers can go back to school to get trained in any of the related fields (radiologic technologists, nuclear medicine technologists, diagnostic sonographers, or medical equipment repairers).
Medical equipment repairers	Repairers can go back to school and obtain a bachelor's degree in order to work on more specialized equipment or obtain a higher pay rate. They can also climb the ranks in management or other areas.
Clinical research assistants	Assistants can work their way up into coordinator positions.
Clinical research coordinators	Coordinators can work their way up to the level of intermediary auditors who oversee many sites.
Dispensing opticians	With further training and education, opticians can become lab technicians, technologists, ophthalmologists, or optometrists.
Ophthalmology lab technicians	With further training and education, lab technicians can become office technicians, opticians, ophthalmologists, or optometrists.
Ophthalmology technicians	With further training and education, technicians can become lab technicians, ophthalmologists, or optometrists.

Occupational health and safety technicians	Technicians can go back to school to become specialists.
Occupational health and safety specialists	Specialists can go back to school for a master's degree to work in more specialized industries like industrial hygiene, health physics, or other areas.
Dental assistants	Assistants can return to school to become either hygienists or dentists.
Dental hygienists	Hygienists can become instructors or researchers, or move into various public health clinics or administrative positions.
Dental laboratory technicians	Lab technicians can go to school to become dental assistants, hygienists, or dentists.
Medical appliance technicians	Technicians can return to school to become prosthetists.
Veterinary technicians	Technicians can return to school to become veterinarians.

also find out if your company pays for advanced training. If it does, definitely take advantage of this. The more certifications and knowledge you have, the better. This will give you more skills to market later on and more opportunities for advancement. It will also lead to job security at your present position.

In the end, whether or not you are a success in the field of medical technology will be entirely up to you.

Take advantage of every opportunity to learn and grow in the field. But above all, enjoy what you do. After all, there's nothing worse than dreading going to work every day. Bringing a bad attitude to work will make the environment a drag for you, your colleagues, and the patients.

Find within yourself a passion for what you do. This passion will not only make your everyday experience on the job more enjoyable but will also help you climb that career ladder more quickly and effectively. As veterinarian technician Kaylene Jacobsen puts it, "Why not work at a job that you love? For me, I love what I do, and that makes going to work every day a lot easier and more enjoyable."

GLOSSARY

biology The science of life or of living matter.

cardiologists Physicians who specialize in the heart and diseases related to this organ.

cardiovascular Pertaining to the heart and its arteries and veins.

clinical Dealing with patients in a real-life setting rather than just studying about diseases and problems in a classroom.

diagnostic Analyzing or detecting something.

dispensing Distributing or handing out something.

nuclear Relating to energy that is released in nuclear fission or fusion.

occupational Relating to a job or profession.

oncologist The branch of medicine that deals with cancerous tumors.

ophthalmologist A medical doctor (MD) who specializes in treating eye disorders and diseases and who can also do eye surgeries.

ophthalmology The branch of medicine that deals with the study and treatment of eye disorders and diseases.

optometrist A doctor of optometry (OD) who examines eyes for visual defects, impairments, and other problems.

progressives Representatives of a political reform movement that reached its height in the early 1900s and favored changes in social, political, and economic policy.

radioactive Spontaneous emission of radiation from a radioactive substance (namely alpha particles, nucleons, electrons, and gamma rays).

respiratory Related to breathing or the lungs and airway.

technical school A school that teaches applied sciences and industrial and mechanical arts.

technician A person who is adept at the technical details of a subject.

technology The making, use of, and knowledge of machines, equipment, and tools.

tumor An abnormal growth of tissues that are either cancerous or noncancerous.

ventilator A machine that pushes oxygen through the lungs of a patient who is having difficulty breathing on his or her own.

American Association of Medical Assistants (AAMA)
20 North Wacker Drive, Suite 1575
Chicago, IL 60606
(312) 899-1500
Web site: http://aama-ntl.org
The AAMA is the professional association for medical
    assistants. It provides certification and other services.

American Association of Medical Dosimetrists (AAMD)
2201 Cooperative Way, Suite 600
Herndon, VA 20171
(703) 677-8071
Web site: http://medicaldosimetry.org/index.cfm
The American Association of Medical Dosimetrists is an
    international society established to promote and support
    the medical dosimetry profession. It provides opportuni-
    ties for education, a forum for professional interaction,
    and a representative voice in the health care community.

American Medical Technologists (AMT)
10700 West Higgins Road, Suite 150
Rosemont, IL 60018
(847) 823-5169
Web site: http://www.americanmedtech.org
The AMT is the certification agency and membership
    society that provides services for a number of allied
    health professional specialties.

The American Occupational Therapy Association (AOTA)
4720 Montgomery Lane

Bethesda, MD 20814
(301) 652-2682
Web site: http://www.aota.org
The AOTA provides certification and other services to pro-
    fessionals and students in the occupational therapy field.

American Registry of Radiologic Technologists (ARRT)
1255 Northland Drive
St. Paul, MN 55120
(651) 687-0048
Web site: https://www.arrt.org
ARRT is the world's largest credentialing organization that
    seeks to ensure high-quality patient care in medical imag-
    ing, interventional procedures, and radiation therapy. It
    tests and certifies technologists and administers continuing
    education and ethics requirements for their annual registra-
    tion. ARRT promotes high standards of patient care by
    recognizing qualified individuals in medical imaging,
    interventional procedures, and radiation therapy.

American Society of Radiologic Technologists (ASRT)
15000 Central Avenue SE
Albuquerque, NM 87123-3909
(800) 444-2778
(505) 298-4500
Web site: http://www.asrt.org
The mission of the ASRT is to advance the medical imag-
    ing and radiation therapy profession and to enhance
    the quality of patient care. It seeks to be the premier
    professional association for the medical imaging and
    radiation therapy community through education, advo-
    cacy, and research.

Canadian Medical Association (CMA)
1867 Alta Vista Drive
Ottawa, ON K1G 5W8
Canada
(888) 855-2555
Web site: http://www.cma.ca
The CMA is an association of physicians that advocates
   on the behalf of its members and the public.

Commission on Accreditation of Allied Health Educational
   Programs (CAAHEP)
1361 Park Street
Clearwater, FL 33756
(727) 210-2350
Web site: http://www.caahep.org
CAAHEP provides accreditation to educational programs
   in health science professions. In addition, it offers
   information for students on accredited programs.

ExploreHealthCareers.org
American Dental Education Association
1400 K Street NW, Suite 1100
Washington, DC 20005
(202) 289-7201 or (347) 365-9253
Web site: http://explorehealthcareers.org
ExploreHealthCareers.org is a free multidisciplinary Web
   site designed to explain the array of health professions
   and provide easy access to students seeking information about health careers. This Web site is a joint
   initiative involving national foundations, professional
   associations, health career advisers, educational
   institutions, and college students.

MEDEC
405 The West Mall, Suite 900
Toronto, ON M9C 5J1
Canada
(416) 620-1915
(866) 58-MEDEC (586-3332)
Web site: http://www.medec.org/en
MEDEC speaks for Canada's medical technology com-
    panies in advocating for a responsive, safe, and
    sustainable health care system that is enabled by the
    adoption and use of medical technology.

National Association for Home Care and Hospice (NAHC)
228 Seventh Street SE
Washington, DC 20003
(202) 547-7424
Web site: http://nahc.org
The NAHC is a trade association representing the inter-
    ests and concerns of home care agencies, hospices,
    and home care aide organizations. It also provides
    certification and accreditation programs for members.

Web Sites

Due to the changing nature of Internet links, Rosen
Publishing has developed an online list of Web sites
related to the subject of this book. This site is updated
regularly. Please use this link to access this list:

http://www.rosenlinks.com/HCC/Tech

Ancowitz, Nancy. *Self-Promotion for Introverts: The Quiet Guide to Getting Ahead.* New York, NY: McGraw-Hill, 2010.

Barker, Geoff. *Health and Social Care Careers.* Mankato, MN: AMICUS, 2011.

Beshara, Tony. *Job Search Solution The Ultimate System for Finding a Great Job Now!* New York, NY: American Management Association, 2012.

Brezina, Corona. *Getting a Job in Health Care* (Job Basics: Getting the Job You Need). New York, NY: Rosen Publishing, 2014.

Farr, Michael. *Quick Résumé & Cover Letter Book: Write and Use an Effective Resume in Just One Day.* Indianapolis, IN: JIST Publishing, 2008.

Ferguson. *Medical Technicians and Technologists* (Careers in Focus). New York, NY: Ferguson, 2009.

Freeman, Brian. *The Ultimate Guide to Choosing a Medical Specialty.* 3rd ed. New York, NY: McGraw Hill Companies, 2013.

Fry, Ron. *101 Great Answers to the Toughest Interview Questions.* Boston, MA: Course Technology PTR, 2009.

Fry, Ron. *101 Smart Questions to Ask on Your Interview.* Boston, MA: Course Technology PTR, 2009.

Garfinkle, Joel A. *Getting Ahead: Three Steps to Take Your Career to the Next Level.* Hoboken, NJ: John Wiley & Sons, 2011.

Glickman, Jodi. *Great on the Job: What to Say, How to Say It: The Secrets of Getting Ahead.* New York, NY: St. Martin's Press, 2011.

Gurley, La Verne Tolley. *Introduction to Radiologic Technology*. Maryland Heights, MD: Elsevier, Mosby, 2011.

McMurray, Patrick. *Study Skills Essentials: Oxford Graduates Reveal Their Study Tactics, Essay Secrets, and Exam Advice*. Holywood, Northern Ireland: Effective Study Skills Publications, 2012.

Muchnick, Cynthia C. *The Everything Guide to Study Skills: Strategies, Tips, and Tools You Need to Succeed in School!* Avon, MA: Adams Media, 2011.

Newport, Cal. *So Good They Can't Ignore You: Why Skills Trump Passion in the Quest for Work You Love*. New York, NY: Business Plus, 2012.

Paul, Kevin. *Study Smarter, Not Harder: Use the Genius Inside You*. Bellingham, WA: Self-Counsel Press, 2009.

Peterson's. *Vocational & Technical Schools East: More Than 2,300 Vocational Schools East of the Mississippi River* (Peterson's Vocational and Technical Schools East). Lawrenceville, NJ: Peterson's, 2009.

Peterson's. *Vocational & Technical Schools West: More Than 2,300 Vocational Schools West of the Mississippi River* (Peterson's Vocational and Technical Schools West). Lawrenceville, NJ: Peterson's, 2009.

Shatkin, Laurence, and Michael Farr. *Top 100 Careers Without a Four-Year Degree*. Indianapolis, IN: JIST Works, 2012.

Sunday, Nina. *Brainpower Smart Study: How to Study Effectively Using a Tested and Proven 8-Step Method*. Sydney, Australia: Brainpower Training 2011.

Teach, Andy. *From Graduation to Corporation: The Practical Guide to Climbing the Corporate Ladder*

One Rung at a Time. Bloomington, IN: Author
House, 2012.
Wilson, Patrick. *Health IT JumpStart: The Best First Step
Toward an IT Career in Health Information Technology.*
Indianapolis, IN: John Wiley & Sons, 2012.
Wischnitzer, Saul, and Edith Wischnitzer. *Top 100 Health-
Care Careers: Your Complete Guidebook to Training
and Jobs in Allied Health, Nursing, Medicine, and
More.* 3rd ed. Indianapolis, IN: JIST Works, 2011.
Yate, Martin. *Knock 'Em Dead: The Ultimate Job Search
Guide.* Avon, MA: Adams Media, 2011.

BIBLIOGRAPHY

AAMI. "Becoming a Biomedical Equipment Technician (BMET)" (Video). YouTube.com. February 24, 2010. Retrieved February 2013 (http://www.youtube.com /watch?v=ZG81JoEZDVc).

Altom, Coleen. Personal interview with author, January 2013.

American Medical Association. *Health Care Careers Directory 2011–2012*. 39th ed. Chicago, IL: American Medical Association, 2011.

Anderson, Hannah. Personal interview with author, January 2013.

Blanchard, John. Personal interview with author, January 2013.

Brown, Ciera. Personal interview with author, February 2013.

Bureau of Labor Statistics. "Dental Assistant." *Occupational Outlook Handbook*, June 26, 2012. Retrieved February 2013 (http://www.bls.gov/ooh/healthcare/dental-assistants.htm).

Bureau of Labor Statistics. "Dental Hygienist." *Occupational Outlook Handbook*, March 29, 2012. Retrieved February 2013 (http://www.bls.gov/ooh/healthcare /dental-hygienists.htm).

Bureau of Labor Statistics. "Dental Laboratory Technicians." *Occupational Outlook Handbook*, June 26, 2012. Retrieved February 2013 (http://www.bls.gov/ooh/ production/dental-laboratory-technicians.htm).

Bureau of Labor Statistics. "Dispensing Optician." *Occupational Outlook Handbook*, March 29, 2012.

Retrieved February 2013 (http://www.bls.gov/ooh/healthcare/opticians-dispensing.htm).

Bureau of Labor Statistics. "Employment Projections—2010–20." U.S. Department of Labor, February 1, 2012. Retrieved February 2013 (http://www.bls.gov/news.release/pdf/ecopro.pdf).

Bureau of Labor Statistics. "Medical and Clinical Laboratory Technologists and Technicians." Occupational Outlook Handbook, April 6, 2012. Retrieved February 2013 (http://www.bls.gov/ooh/healthcare/medical-and-clinical-laboratory-technologists-and-technicians.htm).

Bureau of Labor Statistics. "Medical Appliance Technicians." Occupational Outlook Handbook, June 26, 2012. Retrieved February 2013 (http://www.bls.gov/ooh/production/medical-appliance-technicians.htm).

Bureau of Labor Statistics. "Medical Equipment Preparers." Occupational Outlook Handbook, May 25, 2012. Retrieved February 2013 (http://www.bls.gov/ooh/About/Data-for-Occupations-Not-Covered-in-Detail.htm#healthcareoccupations).

Bureau of Labor Statistics. "Medical Equipment Repairers." Occupational Outlook Handbook, March 29, 2012. Retrieved February 2013 (http://www.bls.gov/ooh/installation-maintenance-and-repair/medical-equipment-repairers.htm).

Bureau of Labor Statistics. "Nuclear Medicine Technologists." Occupational Outlook Handbook, March 29, 2012. Retrieved February 2013 (http://www.bls.gov/ooh/healthcare/nuclear-medicine-technologists.htm).

Bureau of Labor Statistics. "Occupational Health and Safety Technicians." *Occupational Outlook Handbook*, April 10, 2012. Retrieved February 2013 (http://www.bls.gov/ooh/healthcare/occupational-health-and-safety-technicians.htm).

Bureau of Labor Statistics. "Ophthalmology Lab Technician." *Occupational Outlook Handbook*, June 26, 2012. Retrieved February 2013 (http://www.bls.gov/ooh/production/ophthalmic-laboratory-technicians.htm).

Bureau of Labor Statistics. "Radiation Therapists." *Occupational Outlook Handbook*, April 6, 2012. Retrieved February 2013 (http://www.bls.gov/ooh/healthcare/radiation-therapists.htm).

Bureau of Labor Statistics. "Radiologic Technologists." *Occupational Outlook Handbook*, March 29, 2012. Retrieved February 2013 (http://www.bls.gov/ooh/healthcare/radiologic-technologists.htm#tab-1).

Bureau of Labor Statistics. "Respiratory Therapists." *Occupational Outlook Handbook*, April 6, 2012. Retrieved February 2013 (http://www.bls.gov/ooh/healthcare/respiratory-therapists.htm).

CDC. "Achievements in Public Health, 1900–1999: Improvements in Workplace Safety—United States, 1990–1999." *Morbidity and Mortality Weekly Report*, June 11, 1999. Retrieved February 2013 (http://www.cdc.gov/mmwr/pdf/wk/mm4822.pdf).

Commission on Accreditation of Allied Health Education Programs. "Cardiovascular Technology." Retrieved February 2013 (http://www.caahep.org/Content.aspx?ID=21).

Curtis, Kent. Personal interview with author, January 2013.

Damp, Dennis V. *Health Care Job Explosion! High Growth Health Care Careers and Job Locators*. McKees Rocks, PA: Bookhaven Press, 2006.

Davis, Chris. Personal interview with author, January 2013.

Ellis, Amber. Personal interview with author, February 2013.

ExploreHealthCareers.org. "Cardiovascular Technologist /Technician." Retrieved February 2013 (http:// explorehealthcareers.org/en/Career/30 /Cardiovascular_TechnologistTechnician#Tab= Overview).

Ferguson. *The Top 100: The Fastest-Growing Careers for the 21st Century*. 5th ed. New York, NY: Facts On File, 2011.

Field, Shelly. *Career Opportunities in Health Care*. New York, NY: Ferguson, 2007.

Griffith, Aundrea. Personal interview with author, January 2013.

Guerrero, Carla Leon. Personal interview with author, January 2013.

Healthcare Careers. "Medical Equipment Preparers." Retrieved February 2013 (http://www.healthcareca-reers.org/medical-equipment-preparer).

Jacobsen, Kaylene. Personal interview with author, January 2013.

Jaworowski, Lauren. Personal interview with author, February 2013.

Jeter, Cassie Olpin. Personal interview with author, January 2013.

Jones, Brittany. Personal interview with author, January 2013.

Jones, Gary. Personal Interview with author, February 2013.

Kacen, Alex. *Opportunities in Allied Health Careers.* New York, NY: McGraw-Hill, 2005.

Kimball, Cheryl. *Start Your Health Care Career.* Irvine, CA: Entrepreneur Press, 2007.

MedlinePlus. "EEG." Retrieved February 2013 (http://www.nlm.nih.gov/medlineplus/ency/article/003931.htm).

Moore, Kristina Hudson. Personal interview with author, January 2013.

O*Net Online. "Medical Equipment Preparers." Retrieved February 2013 (http://www.onetonline.org/link/summary/31-9093.00).

O*Net Online. "Medical Equipment Repairers." Retrieved February 2013 (http://www.onetonline.org/link/summary/49-9062.00).

Reynolds, Wendy. Personal interview with author, January 2013.

Stratford, S.J. *Ferguson Field Guides to Finding a New Career: Health Care.* New York, NY: Checkmark Books, 2009.

VGM editors. *Resumes for Health and Medical Careers.* 3rd ed. Chicago, IL: VGM Career Books, 2004.

WebMD. "Electrocardiogram." Retrieved February 2013 (http://www.webmd.com/heart-disease/electrocardiogram).

Weeks, Zona R. *Opportunities in Occupational Therapy Careers.* New York, NY: McGraw Hill, 2007.

Zedlitz, Robert H. *How to Get a Job in Health Care.* Clifton Park, NY: Delmar Learning, 2003.

INDEX

About the Author

Amie Jane Leavitt is an accomplished author and researcher who has written more than fifty books for young people, has contributed to online and print media, and has worked as a consultant, writer, and editor for numerous educational publishing and assessment companies. Her networking and researching skills allow her to locate professional and expert interview subjects to consult with for her nonfiction titles, as she did for *Jump-Starting a Career in Medical Technology*. She graduated from Brigham Young University and has since taught all subjects and grade levels in both public and private schools. To see a listing of Ms. Leavitt's current projects and published works, check out her Web site at www.amiejaneleavitt.com.

Photo Credits